e Your Own Best Friend Forever!

WRITTEN AND ILLUSTRATED BY

Gary Robinson

FEATURING JAYLA ROSE

7th Generation

Summertown, Tennessee

We chose to print this title on paper certified by The Forest Stewardship Council® (FSC®), a global, not-for-profit organization dedicated to the promotion of responsible forest management worldwide.

Printed in China

7th Generation
Book Publishing Company
PO Box 99, Summertown, TN 38483
888-260-8458
bookpubco.com
nativevoicesbooks.com

ISBN: 978-1-939053-34-3

26 25 24 23 22 21   1 2 3 4 5 6 7 8 9

ACKNOWLEDGMENTS

I want to first thank my daughter, Anisa,
for her help in fine-tuning the text of this book
and for Landon, my grandson.

I also want to thank Jayla's parents, John and Lila Ormond,
for giving her permission to work with me on this book.

Of course, I thank Jayla for her outgoing nature and for speaking the words
"I believe in myself," which inspired this book.

And last but not least, I thank Lola, my best friend and love for the rest of my life,
for her love and for igniting the spark that led to this book..

Be Your Own Best Friend

FOREVER!

Okay, girls,
my name is Jayla,
and I've got something
to say!

I've learned to take pride
in who I am
as an African American,
Native American,
Asian American, and Latina girl.
Yes, I'm all of these.

I believe in myself, and
I believe you can
believe in yourself too!
All you need to do is
follow a few simple steps. . . .

There's a voice inside your head
that talks to you all the time.
I have one. You have one.
What does your voice say to you?

Does it say stuff like this?

Your hair is too curly.

Your skin is too dark.

You are different and weird.

You're not good enough.

That's called negative self-talk.

It's not good for you,
and you don't have to listen to it!

If your inner voice says those negative things,
TURN IT OFF!
If your friends tell you those negative things,
GET NEW FRIENDS!

If a TV program says those things,

CHANGE THE CHANNEL!

If a book says those things,

TURN THE PAGE!

If someone online says those things,

BLOCK THEM!

It's time to replace that negative talk
with Positive Talk, inside and out.
It's time to write your own songs
and tell yourself your own truth.
In other words, it's time to
BE YOUR OWN BEST FRIEND!

When you look in the mirror
each morning and night,
reject the voice of self-doubt and self-hate.
Turn UP the voice of love and light.

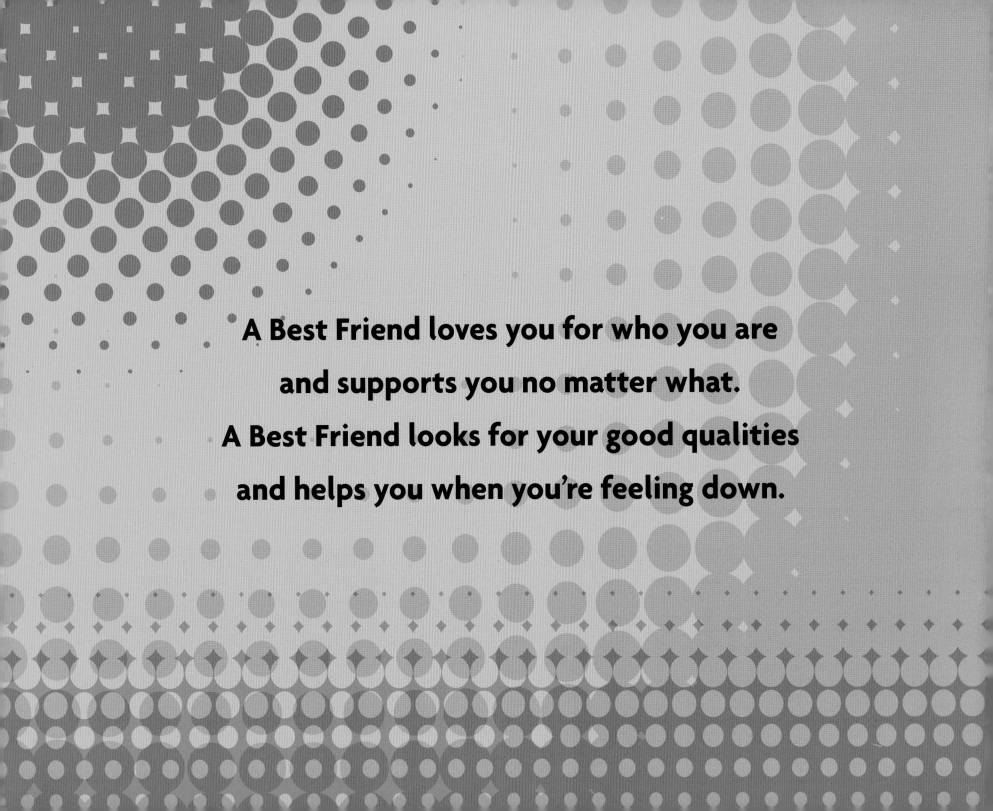

A Best Friend loves you for who you are
and supports you no matter what.
A Best Friend looks for your good qualities
and helps you when you're feeling down.

To be your own Best Friend,

practice positive self-talk like this:

My brain is smart.

My muscles are strong.

My heart is loving.

My whole self is beautiful.

I am enough just the way I am.

If someone tries to make fun
of your skin, hair, body, culture, or beliefs,
remember that those are
what make you special and unique.
They make you, YOU!
Those are your strengths,
not your weaknesses.

BE YOU

Make friends with kids
who believe in themselves
and know they are beautiful too—
kids who also know they have
the power to change the world
and make it a better place.

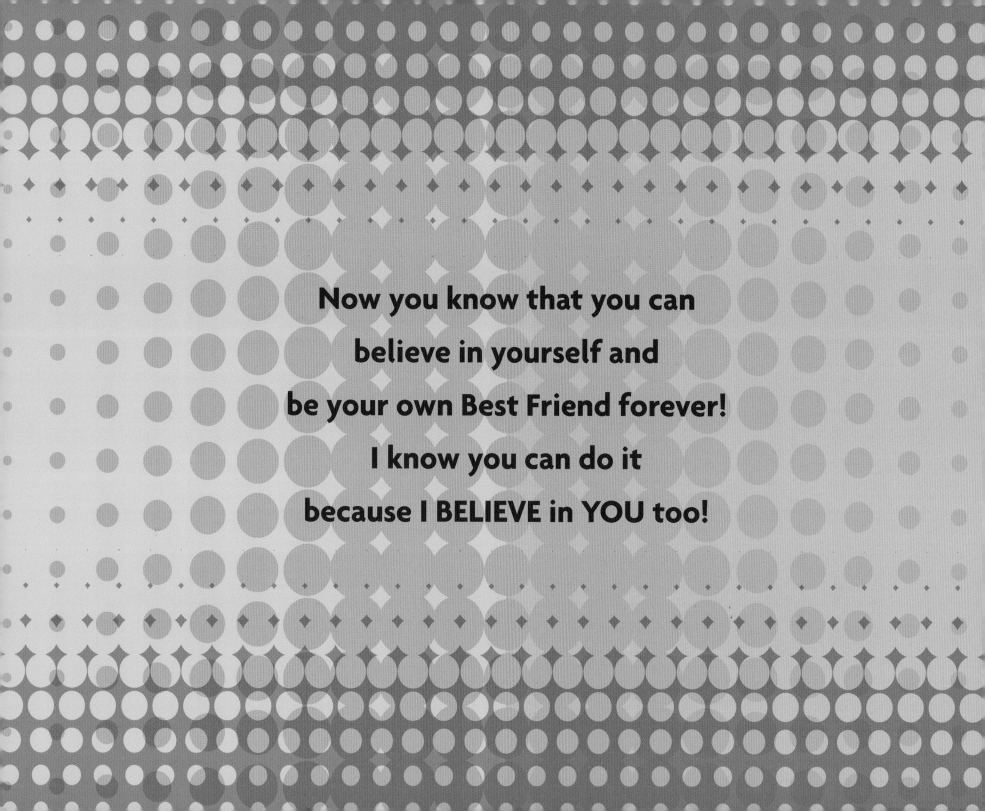

Now you know that you can

believe in yourself and

be your own Best Friend forever!

I know you can do it

because I BELIEVE in YOU too!

This is not the end.

It's only the beginning—

the new beginning of your own life.

A life filled with endless possibilities!

Believing in yourself is the first step.

All you have to do is take it.

Jayla Rose is a real girl living in central California with her mom, dad, and brother.

Jayla regularly says she believes in herself, and she knows you can too!

Thanks for your inspiration, Jayla!

Gary Robinson is an award-winning writer and film-maker of Choctaw/Cherokee descent. Gary has worked most of his life to create Native American content in dozens of Native American educational, informational, and documentary television projects. He is the author of sixteen books, including eight PathFinders teen novels. He lives in Santa Ynez, California. For more information, visit his website at tribaleyeproductions.com.

OTHER WORKS BY THE AUTHOR

Native American Night Before Christmas

Native American Twelve Days of Christmas

Thunder on the Plains

Tribal Journey

Little Brother of War

Son Who Returns

Abnormal; Paranormal; Supranormal (a three-book series)

Standing Strong

From Warriors to Soldiers

The Language of Victory: Code Talkers of World War I and World War II

Lands of Our Ancestors (books 1–3)

Tribal Sovereignty

Native Legacy: Indigenous Innovations and Contributions to the World

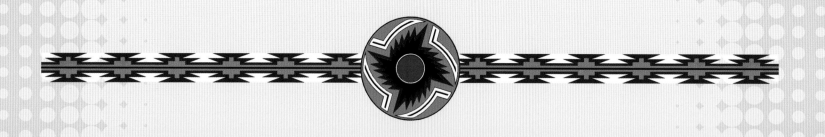